First Facts®

Spotlight on the Continents

SPOTLIGHT ON

ASIA

by A. R. Schaefer

CAPSTONE PRESS
a capstone imprint

First Facts is published by Capstone Press,
151 Good Counsel Drive, P.O. Box 669, Mankato, Minnesota 56002.
www.capstonepub.com

Books published by Capstone Press are manufactured with paper
containing at least 10 percent post-consumer waste.

Library of Congress Cataloging-in-Publication Data
Schaefer, A. R. (Adam Richard), 1976–
 Spotlight on Asia / by A.R. Schaefer.
   p. cm.—(First facts. Spotlight on the continents)
 Summary: "An introduction to Asia including climate, landforms, plants, animals,
and people"—Provided by publisher.
 Includes bibliographical references and index.
 ISBN 978-1-4296-6623-7 (library binding)
 1. Asia—Juvenile literature. I. Title.
 DS5.S24 2011
 950—dc22   2010037109

Editorial Credits
Lori Shores, editor; Gene Bentdahl, designer; Laura Manthe, production specialist

Photo Credits
DigitalVision, 14 (bottom, top right)
Flat Earth Collection, 1
Shutterstock/Asia Glab, 20; Hugh Lansdown, 9 (bottom right); LiteChoices, 19;
    Oleg Kozlov, 9 (top); Peter Wey, 14 (top left); Photobank, 13 (left); salajean, 12;
    Sam DCruz, 16; Seti, 9 (bottom left); Superpetya, cover; Tracing Tea, 13 (right);
    Tupungato, 18

Artistic Effects
Shutterstock/seed

Essential content terms are **bold** and are defined at the bottom of the page
where they first appear.

Printed in the United States of America in Melrose Park, Illinois.
092010   005935LKS11

TABLE OF CONTENTS

CONTINENTS OF THE WORLD

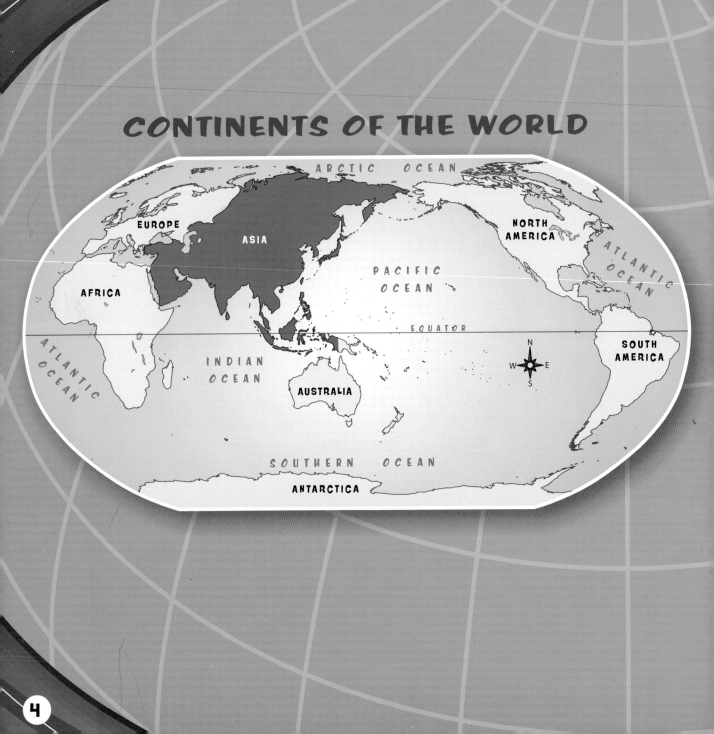

ASIA

Asia is the biggest **continent** in the world. This landmass stretches across more than 17 million square miles (44 million square kilometers).

Asia has the largest population of any continent. About three-fifths of the world's people live here. Across this giant continent, Asia's people are as varied as the land.

continent—one of Earth's seven large landmasses

FAST FACTS ABOUT
ASIA

⊕ **Population:** Almost 4.2 billion

⊕ **Number of countries:** 50

⊕ **Largest cities:** Tokyo, Japan; Mumbai, India; Seoul, South Korea; Jakarta, Indonesia; Shanghai, China

⊕ **Longest river:** Yangtze River, 3,900 miles (6,276 kilometers)

⊕ **Highest point:** Mount Everest, 29,035 feet (8,850 meters) tall

⊕ **Lowest point:** Dead Sea, 1,385 feet (422 meters) below sea level

COUNTRIES OF ASIA

ARCTIC OCEAN

RUSSIA

RUSSIA
(EUROPE)

EUROPE

KAZAKHSTAN

AZERBAIJAN

KYRGYZSTAN

MONGOLIA

GEORGIA

TAJIKISTAN

NORTH
KOREA

ARMENIA

UZBEKISTAN

JAPAN

TURKEY

TURKMENISTAN

CHINA

SOUTH
KOREA

CYPRUS

SYRIA

IRAN

AFGHANISTAN

BHUTAN

PACIFIC
OCEAN

LEBANON

IRAQ

BAHRAIN

PAKISTAN

NEPAL

ISRAEL

QATAR

TAIWAN

JORDAN

KUWAIT

MYANMAR

SAUDI
ARABIA

INDIA

LAOS

PHILIPPINES

THAILAND

UNITED
ARAB
EMIRATES

VIETNAM

OMAN

CAMBODIA

BANGLADESH

YEMEN

BRUNEI

MALDIVES

SRI
LANKA

MALAYSIA

PAPUA
NEW GUINEA

AFRICA

Kilometers
500   1000
0   620
Miles

SINGAPORE

INDONESIA

EAST
TIMOR

N
W   E
S

INDIAN
OCEAN

AUSTRALIA

7

CLIMATE

Asia's **climate** ranges from the cold, snowy north to the hot, rainy south. Northern areas have snow all year. Central Asia has both cold mountain and hot desert climates. Deserts also cover areas of southwestern Asia.

Southeast Asia has long periods of wet weather. Strong seasonal winds, called monsoons, bring heavy rainfall to Southeast Asia's **rain forests**.

climate—the usual weather that occurs in a place
rain forest—a thick forest where a great deal of rain falls

LANDFORMS OF ASIA

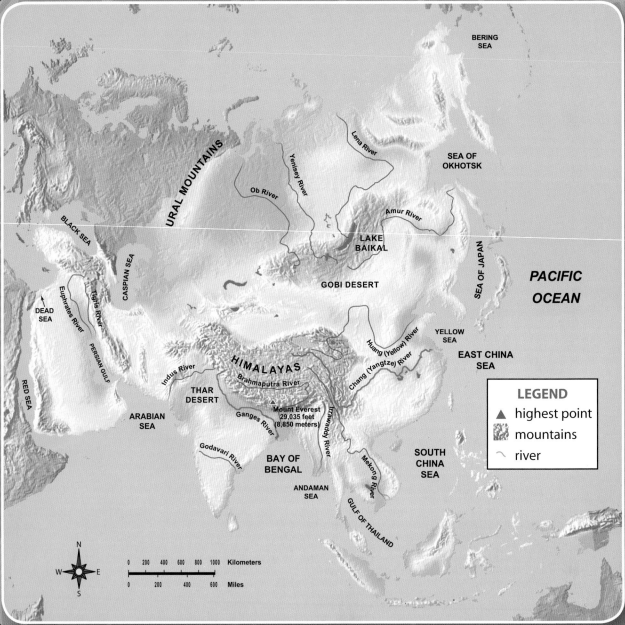

BERING SEA

SEA OF OKHOTSK

Lena River

Amur River

URAL MOUNTAINS

Yenisey River

Ob River

LAKE BAIKAL

SEA OF JAPAN

PACIFIC OCEAN

BLACK SEA

CASPIAN SEA

GOBI DESERT

YELLOW SEA

EAST CHINA SEA

DEAD SEA

Euphrates River

Tigris River

PERSIAN GULF

Huang (Yellow) River

Chang (Yangtze) River

HIMALAYAS

Indus River

Brahmaputra River

RED SEA

THAR DESERT

Mount Everest 29,035 feet (8,850 meters)

Ganges River

Irrawaddy River

ARABIAN SEA

Godavari River

BAY OF BENGAL

ANDAMAN SEA

Mekong River

SOUTH CHINA SEA

GULF OF THAILAND

LEGEND
▲ highest point

🗻 mountains

⌒ river

N
W E
S

| 0 | 200 | 400 | 600 | 800 | 1000 | Kilometers |

| 0 | 200 | 400 | 600 | Miles |

LANDFORMS

Asia has the world's highest and lowest points. Mount Everest is the world's tallest mountain at 29,035 feet (8,850 meters) tall. The salty Dead Sea is the lowest point on Earth at 1,385 feet (422 m) below sea level.

People depend on Asia's rivers and lakes. The Yangtze and Ganges rivers are used to water crops. The Caspian Sea provides fish and oil.

PLANTS

Thousands of plants grow in Asia. Colorful wildflowers and tall grasses cover central Asia. Fir and pine forests grow in the south.

Plants that grow in the warm, wet climate of southeast Asia are sold worldwide. Much of the world's tea, rubber, and bamboo grow there. Farmers also grow rice, wheat, and cotton in these areas.

ANIMALS

Thick fur keeps foxes and reindeer warm in northern Asia. Snow leopards catch sheep and goats in the mountains. Orangutans swing from rain forest trees. On the ground, elephants munch on plants.

Some **endangered** animals only live in Asia. Tigers and giant pandas make their homes in Asia's wilderness.

endangered—at risk of dying out

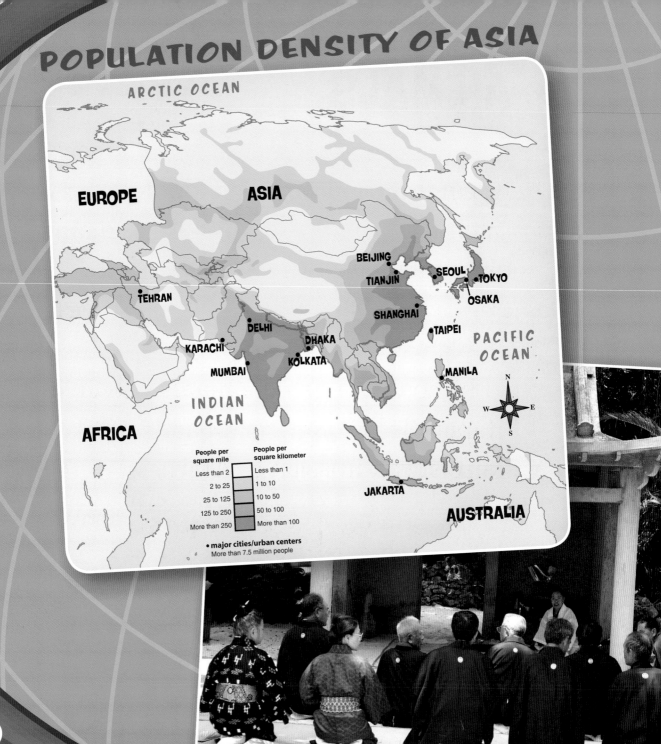

POPULATION DENSITY OF ASIA

ARCTIC OCEAN

EUROPE

ASIA

AFRICA

TEHRAN

KARACHI

MUMBAI

DELHI

DHAKA

KOLKATA

BEIJING

TIANJIN

SEOUL

TOKYO

OSAKA

SHANGHAI

TAIPEI

MANILA

PACIFIC OCEAN

INDIAN OCEAN

JAKARTA

AUSTRALIA

People per square mile	People per square kilometer
Less than 2	Less than 1
2 to 25	1 to 10
25 to 125	10 to 50
125 to 250	50 to 100
More than 250	More than 100

• major cities/urban centers
More than 7.5 million people

PEOPLE

People practice many religions in Asia. Hinduism has the largest number of followers. Many Asians also practice Islam or Buddhism.

Of Asia's many languages, Chinese has the most speakers with more than 1 billion. Millions of Asians speak Japanese and Korean. Many Asians also speak Russian or Arabic.

LIVING IN ASIA

In Asian cities, many people live in apartment buildings. They have many choices of clothing and food. Most people wear modern clothing.

In rural areas, people have fewer choices. They live in small wood or mud homes. They grow rice and vegetables to eat. People often make their own clothing, including traditional outfits.

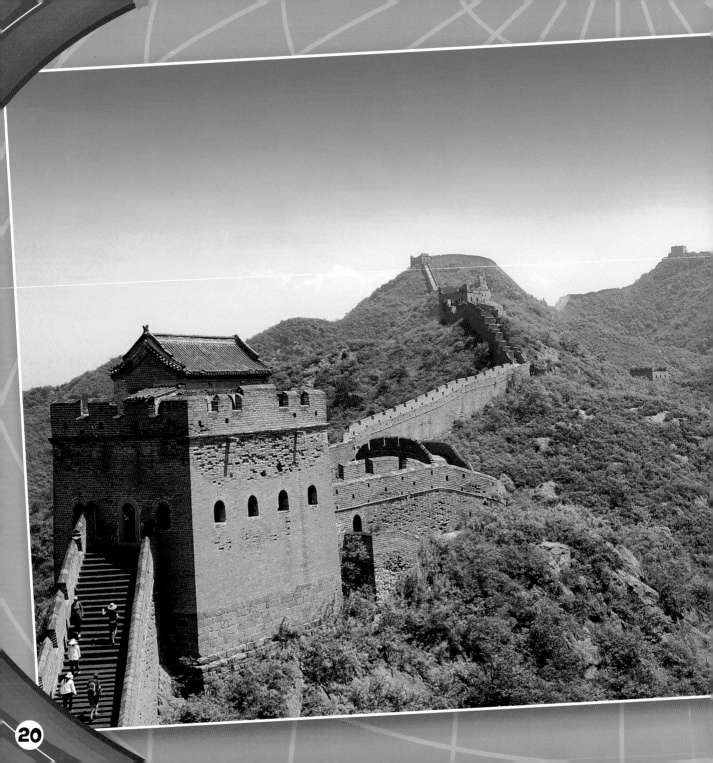

ASIA AND THE WORLD

Asia is called the cradle of civilization. Asians were the first to farm, make laws, and create cities. The first paper and writing system also came from Asia.

Asian **culture** has also influenced the world. All of the world's main religions began on this continent.

culture—a people's way of life, ideas, customs, and traditions

GLOSSARY

climate (KLY-muht)—the usual weather that occurs in a place

continent (KAHN-tuh-nuhnt)—one of Earth's seven large landmasses

culture (KUHL-chuhr)—a people's way of life, ideas, customs, and traditions

endangered (in-DAYN-juhrd)—at risk of dying out

rain forest (RAYN FOR-ist)—a thick forest where a great deal of rain falls

READ MORE

Ganeri, Anita. *Asia.* Exploring Continents. Chicago: Heinemann Library, 2007.

Kalman, Bobbie, and Rebecca Sjonger. *Explore Asia.* Explore the Continents. New York: Crabtree Pub. Co., 2007.

Law, Felicia. *Atlas of Southwest and Central Asia.* World Atlases. Minneapolis: Picture Window Books, 2008.

INTERNET SITES

FactHound offers a safe, fun way to find Internet sites related to this book. All of the sites on FactHound have been researched by our staff.

Here's all you do:

Visit *www.facthound.com*

Type in this code: 9781429666237

Check out projects, games and lots more at
www.capstonekids.com

INDEX